Joseph's Journey
Volume 2

Poetry of
Hope, Help, Healing
and Humor

Psychological Concepts Expressed in Poetry

Joseph's Journey
Volume 2

Poetry of
Hope, Help, Healing
and Humor

Psychological Concepts
Expressed in Poetry

by

Joseph Fram

Everlasting Publishing
Yakima, Washington, USA

Joseph's Journey
Volume 2

Psychological Concepts
Expressed in Poetry

by
Joseph Fram

Library of Congress Control Number:
2006928901

ISBN: 0-9778083-1-9
ISBN-13: 978-0-9778083-1-1

First Edition
Everlasting Publishing
P.O. Box 1061
Yakima, WA 98907

Editor's note:
My dad, an extremely intelligent and also loving and compassionate man, has always been an exemplary example to me, and he taught me many things. Here are three of the most important:
1. Always do your best
2. Never give up hope
3. Love God, and love others with the love of Jesus

He also taught me to look for the humor in the situation, and to experience life with joy every day.

With much love,

Dana

This book is dedicated to my family: my brother, George, my sisters, Helen and Elizabeth, and my children, Dana and Dale; and also, the special woman in my life, Doreen.

Joseph's Journey — Volume 2
Psychological Concepts Expressed in Poetry

STAIRS OF LIFE................................ 1

THE FAMILY................................... 2

AN AMERICAN.................................. 3

MOMENTS IN MY HEART.......................... 4

PENZANCE PIRATE.............................. 5

LOVE IS NEVER LOST........................... 6

SENILITY..................................... 7

PIRATE JOE................................... 8

ROSES IN MY HEART............................ 9

IT'S CHRISTMAS.............................. 10

GOD HAS CALLED ME........................... 11

RUNNING OUT OF TIME......................... 12

I CRY INSIDE................................ 13

NEVER LOST MY DREAM......................... 14

NOW ARE YOU HAPPY........................... 15

DE JA' VU................................... 16

DRIFTING.................................... 17

KINDNESS OF MY MIND......................... 18

BROTHER GEORGE.............................. 19

LOVE FOR CHRISTMAS.......................... 20

HER WORDS................................... 21

MY FATHER'S SON............................. 22

CHRISTMAS I REMEMBER........................ 23

ONE SUMMER NIGHT............................ 24

HARD TIMES.................................. 25

NOT FOR SALE...............................26

MY CHILDREN................................27

NOSES......................................28

NOT ALL GEMS ARE DIAMONDS..................29

FUNNY......................................30

CHRISTMAS IMAGE............................31

DEATH......................................32

EASIER NOW.................................33

LONG GOOD MORNING.........................34

LEADERS TAKE THE BLAME.....................35

HAPPY BIRTHDAY DOREEN.....................36

I'LL WAIT FOR YOU.........................37

LOVE PLUS..................................38

JUST FOR FUN...............................39

MYRNA FAREWELL.............................40

GOD'S RELIGION.............................41

BETTER PLACE DOWN THE ROAD.................42

BITTER WORDS...............................43

CHRISTMAS TIME LOVE.......................44

HOW MANY?..................................45

BEEN LOVED?................................46

GOD'S CHURCH...............................47

IT DOESN'T MATTER NOW.....................48

TIME AND DISTANCE.........................49

MY SAY.....................................50

STAIRS OF LIFE
by
Joseph Fram

SOMETIMES THOSE STAIRS ARE HARD TO CLIMB
SOMETIMES YOU CANNOT CLIMB AT ALL
IT IS HARD TO GET BACK UP
WHEN YOU'RE AT THE TOP AND FALL

SOMETIMES STAIRS ARE JUST TOO HIGH
WHEN THE FIRST STEP'S NOT BEGUN
BUT YOU WILL NEVER REACH THE TOP
UNLESS YOU TAKE THEM ONE BY ONE

TAKE EACH STEP AND TAKE YOUR TIME
IF YOU NEED REST, THEN MAKE A STOP
AND SOMETIMES EVEN ASK YOURSELF
WHAT WILL I FIND UP ON THE TOP?

HOW MUCH HIGHER WILL I CLIMB
THE SET OF STAIRS MAY HAVE NO END
ALWAYS BUILD EACH STEP WITH CARE
SO AT THE TOP THE STAIRS CAN BEND

PLACE A LANDING HERE AND THERE
AT POINTS WHERE YOU ENJOY THE VIEW
SO IF YOU FALL OR IF YOU STOP
THE STAIRS YOU BUILD WILL SEE YOU THROUGH

1

THE FAMILY
by
Joseph Fram

I MET A FAMILY LONG AGO
AT A TIME THAT I WAS SEEKING ONE
FOR MINE HAD FALLEN ALL APART
BUT THIS ONE SEEMED TO HAVE SUCH FUN

THOUGH NOT WAS EASY ALL THE TIME
THEY STUCK TOGETHER ALL THE YEARS
THERE WAS LAUGHTER MOST FOR THEM
BUT ON OCCASION THERE WERE TEARS

ONE OF THE THINGS THAT NEVER CHANGED
WAS ALL THE LOVE THAT THEY EMBRACED
SOME DISAPPROVED THINGS THAT WERE DONE
COULD NEVER HAVE THAT CLOSE LOVE CHASED

THEN WHEN I SAW THEM YESTERDAY
I KNEW THAT THEIR LOVE WAS REAL
FOR IN THEIR HOUSE IT FILLED THE AIR
AND ALL THEY DID JUST HAD THAT FEEL

THEN I KNEW WHAT FAMILY WAS
THEY CONSIDER ALL AS BROTHERS
THEY MEASURE NOT WITH WHAT THEY HAVE
BUT WHAT THEY CAN DO FOR OTHERS

AN AMERICAN
by
Joseph Fram

I AM AN AMERICAN
AND THAT I WILL ALWAYS BE
THERE WILL BE NO SEPARATION
NO MATTER HOW YOU COLOR ME

WHEN MY COUNTRY NEEDS ME
I GO WHERE DUTY CALLS
IF I AM TO KEEP MY FREEDOM
I MUST SERVE BEYOND THESE WALLS

I HAVE SEEN MY FLAG AFLYING
SOMETIMES TATTERED SOMETIMES TORN
STILL IT SAYS I AM AMERICAN
FROM THE DAY THAT I WAS BORN

THERE WILL BE NO STOPPING ME
I MAY BEND BUT NEVER FALL
WITH PRIDE I WILL STAND AGAIN
AND SHARE MY LIBERTY WITH ALL

WHEN YOU HARM MY FELLOW MAN
THERE IS A PRICE TO PAY
JUSTICE WILL CATCH UP WITH YOU
AS AN AMERICAN THAT IS MY WAY

MOMENTS IN MY HEART
by
Joseph Fram

I GUESS I WILL ALWAYS REMEMBER YOU
TOUGH WE MUST REMAIN APART
I KNOW MY SOUL IS FREE FROM YOU
BUT THERE REMAIN MOMENTS IN MY HEART

SOMETIMES A MOMENT COMES TO ME
AT NIGHT WHEN I'M ALONE
OF LAUGHING CHILDREN LOST IN PLAY
WHEN OUR HOUSE WAS STILL A HOME

CHRISTMAS TIME WAS SUCH A JOY
OUR LITTLE GIRL STAYED UP ALL NIGHT
YOU KNOW WHEN SANTA BUILT THAT HOUSE
AND LEFT JUST BEFORE THE CRACK OF LIGHT

OTHER MOMENTS BRING A SMILE
LIKE OUR SON WHO WORKED SO LONG
TO OPEN AT THE OPERA HOUSE
SO WE COULD HEAR HIS SONG

THOUGH ALL THAT MAGIC'S GONE FOR GOOD
MOMENTS IN MY HEART ARE HERE TO STAY
THE ONES I KEEP ARE DEAR TO ME
ALL THE REST I THREW AWAY

PENZANCE PIRATE
by
Joseph Fram

HE SAID HE'D BE A PIRATE
AS HE SAT THE CHURCHYARD STAIR
AND WITH HIS COCKNEY ACCENT
HE TOOK SOME TIME TO SHARE

IN PENZANCE, A PIRATE'S LIFE
IS THE ONLY WAY TO BE
BUT THIS LAD WAS BORN TOO LATE
TO SAIL A GALLEON ON THE SEA

WHEN HE SPOKE, HIS EYES LIT UP
AT ADVENTURES IN HIS MIND
OF GLORY DAYS AND FLAGS AND SHIPS
AND ALL THE TREASURES HE COULD FIND

THOSE AROUND JUST SMILED AT HIM
THEY AGREED A TIME OR TWO
THOUGH THEY WOULD HAVE ALSO GONE
HE WOULD TELL THEM WHAT TO DO

THEN HE STOPPED AND LOOKED AWAY
HE KNEW IT COULD NEVER BE
BUT FOR A MOMENT HE SAILED THAT SHIP
AND HE SHARED THAT RIDE WITH ME

LOVE IS NEVER LOST
by
Joseph Fram

AS A YOUTH I USED TO PRAY
FOR ALL MATERIAL THINGS
IT SEEMED THAT THERE WAS COMFORT IN
MONEY, FURS, AND DIAMOND RINGS

AS I AGED I GOT THOSE THINGS
AND YET, I PRAYED FOR MORE
THE MORE I GOT, THE MORE I FELT
THE WAY I FELT BEFORE

THEN ONE DAY I LOST IT ALL
I THOUGHT THEN 'TWAS THE END
WITH NO ONE THERE TO COMFORT ME
I HAD NO WEALTH TO BUY A FRIEND

I WAS LEFT WITH NOT AT ALL
I ASKED WHY FROM ABOVE
A WHISPER SAID SO TENDERLY
I TOOK WEALTH BUT LEFT YOU LOVE

NOW LOVE IS ALL THAT I HOLD DEAR
I SHARE WITHOUT A COST
THOUGH SOME MAY NEVER UNDERSTAND
A GIVEN LOVE IS NEVER LOST

SENILITY
by
Joseph Fram

I WISH MY MEMORY WORKED TODAY
THE WAY IT DID SO LONG AGO
FOR ALL THE THINGS THAT I KNEW THEN
ARE THINGS NOW THAT I DON'T KNOW

I TRY TO BRING A MEMORY BACK
AND GRASP AT A FLITTING SCENE
AND WHEN I GO TO SOMEPLACE NEW
IS IT SOMEWHERE I'VE ALREADY BEEN?

I CAN CLEARLY SEE MY CHILDHOOD
ALL THE PLACES I WOULD PLAY
BUT IF SOMEONE WERE TO ASK ME
I CAN'T REMEMBER YESTERDAY

I GUESS AS WE GROW OLDER
GOD LEAVES PRECIOUS MEMORIES THERE
AND ERASES ALL THE BAD ONES
HE DOESN'T THINK WE NEED TO SHARE

AND MAYBE IN HIS WISDOM
THROUGH NATURE'S GREAT AGILITY
HE HAS HIDDEN ALL THE BAD ONES
IN A PROCESS CALLED SENILITY

PIRATE JOE
by
Joseph Fram

I AM REALLY QUITE ORDINARY
NEVER ATTRACT ATTENTION WHERE I GO
PEOPLE WALK RIGHT PAST ME
EVEN THOSE I THINK I KNOW

SOME HAVE EVEN SHARED THEIR VIEW
AND SUCH REMARKS THEY MADE
LIKE THE TIME I OVERHEARD THEM SAYING
I'D BE LOST IN A ONE MAN PARADE

BUT SOMETIMES THINGS JUST HAPPEN
AND I NEVER QUESTION WHY
FOR I HAD THE UNFORTUNATE FORTUNE
TO NEED A PATCH OVER MY RIGHT EYE

NOW ALL THE CHILDREN SEE ME
AND STARE AS I GROW NEAR
"MOMMY I SAW A PIRATE"
AS I PASS IS WHAT I HEAR

AS I CHUCKLE I AM THANKFUL
FOR AT LAST I HAVE BEEN SEEN
FOR SOMETHING GOOD HAS HAPPENED
FROM WHAT I ONCE THOUGHT OF AS MEAN

ROSES IN MY HEART
by
Joseph Fram

THAT TOUCH OF BLISS IN OUR YOUNG LOVE
HAS BEEN THERE FROM THE START
RIGHT FROM THE MOMENT WE FIRST MET
I'VE KEPT THOSE PAGES IN MY HEART

ON EVERY PAGE IS WRITTEN LOVE
I SEE YOUR FACE IN EVERY LINE
AND EVERY WORD ON EVERY PAGE
SAYS I AM YOURS AND YOU ARE MINE

IT MATTERS NOT ON ANY PAGE
WHAT WE SAY OR WHAT WE DO
THAT PAGE OF LOVE WILL BE COMPLETE
IF YOU'RE WITH ME AND I WITH YOU

THEN SOMETIMES I WILL GET A ROSE
ON A PAGE ESPECIALLY DEAR
I PRESS THAT ROSE INTO MY HEART
SO I WILL ALWAYS HAVE IT NEAR

TILL NOW MY PAGES ARE ALL FULL
WITH MORE ROSES COMING EVERY DAY
AND I WILL GENTLY CRUSH EACH ROSE
ON PAGES WHERE IT'S MEANT TO STAY

IT'S CHRISTMAS
by
Joseph Fram

CHRISTMAS TIME IS HERE I KNOW
BUT WHERE DID SPRING AND SUMMER GO
MY FRIENDS AND I ARE UNAWARE
OF HOW WE GOT FROM HERE TO THERE

I GUESS WHAT WE HAVE TO DO
IS WATCH MORE CLOSELY YES, YOU TOO
BUT IF WE WATCH AND KEEP THE TIME
WE MAY OVERLOOK OUR FRIENDSHIP SUBLIME

SO WHAT DOES IT MATTER AND WHO KNOWS
WHERE TIME FLIES AND WHERE IT GOES
IF EACH CHRISTMAS YOU CAN SAY
I'M GLAD I MADE IT ALL THIS WAY

AND, OH! YES

MERRY CHRISTMAS

GOD HAS CALLED ME
by
Joseph Fram

A LOOK OF PEACE UPON HIS FACE
A SPECIAL COAT UPON HIS CHEST
SOME MEDALS MARKED HIS LIFE ON EARTH
AND THEY LAID HIM DOWN TO REST

HE SERVED HIS COUNTRY-SERVED IT WELL
HIS ONLY TIME AWAY FROM HOME
HE LIKED HIS LIFE IN THIS SMALL TOWN
SO LOVED BY ALL AND NE'ER ALONE

HE MET ONE GIRL AND FELL IN LOVE
THEN HE MARRIED HER FOR LIFE
THOUGH SHE WAS TAKEN SOON FROM HIM
HE STAYED ALONE, SHE WAS HIS WIFE

HE REARED THE CHILDREN THAT THEY HAD
WITH ALL THE LOVE THAT HE KNEW HOW
AND YOU CAN KNOW HIS LEGACY
BY FINE ADULTS THAT THEY ARE NOW

AS THEY LAID HIM DOWN TO REST
WHEN THEY PLAYED TAPS I SAW HIS FACE
HE SEEMED TO SAY "I'M READY NOW"
FOR GOD HAS CALLED ME TO HIS PLACE

RUNNING OUT OF TIME
by
Joseph Fram

I AM RUNNING OUT OF TIME FOR HATRED
I AM RUNNING OUT OF TIME FOR GREED
I AM RUNNING OUT OF TIME FOR MANY THINGS
AND SEEKING ONLY THINGS I NEED

IN MY YOUTH I HAD A CONFLICT
FOR I WAS TAUGHT TO LOVE AND HATE
JESUS SAID TO LOVE THOSE THAT HATE YOU
MY GOVERNMENT SAID THAT LOVE CAN WAIT

SO I BELIEVED AND WENT TO WAR
IN ANOTHER WORLD I STILL DON'T KNOW
WHEN WE HAD KILLED AND MAIMED ENOUGH
WE WERE TOLD "NOW IT'S TIME TO GO"

FOR ALL WE KILLED A FEW GOT RICH
AND NOW THEY LIVE IN LUXURY
THEY NEVER HAD TO TURN THEIR HEAD
TO WATCH THE DEBT PAID IN MISERY

FOR IT IS GREED THAT DRIVES THESE MEN
ENOUGH IS A WORD THEY DO NOT KNOW
SHOULD SOMEONE ELSE GET A LITTLE MORE
AS IN THE PAST IT'S OFF TO WAR WE GO

BUT NOW I'M RUNNING OUT OF TIME
FOR GREED AND HATE TOWARD FELLOW MAN
I DO NOT WANT TO LEAVE THIS WORLD
NOT REALLY KNOWING WHO I AM

EACH MORN I SAY A SIMPLE PRAYER
THY WILL BE DONE BECOMES MY PLEA
MY TRANSGRESSIONS PLEASE FORGIVE
AND FROM THIS TORMENT SET ME FREE

12

I CRY INSIDE
by
Joseph Fram

I MISS THE HOME
THAT ONCE WAS MINE
I'D BUILT MY CASTLE
PROUD AND FINE

OUR CHILDREN RAISED
MIDST LOVE AND FUN
AND PEACE AT NIGHT
WHEN DAY'S WORK DONE

THE CHILDREN LEFT
WE HAD MORE ROOM TO ROAM
THEY TOOK THE LOVE WITH THEM
NOW JUST A HOUSE, NOT A HOME

THEN ALL THE REST
CAME CRASHING DOWN
WHEN THE WIFE I HAD
BADE ME LEAVE TOWN

WITH FRAGILE BRAVADO NOW
I TRY MY BEST TO HIDE
A FEELING OF HOMELESSNESS
MY TEARLESS EYES CRY INSIDE

NEVER LOST MY DREAM
by
Joseph Fram

LIFE HAS HAD ITS UPS AND DOWNS
I TOOK THEM ALL IN STRIDE
I LET MY DOWNS JUST PETER OUT
MY HIGHS GAVE ME A JOYOUS RIDE

BUT I ALWAYS HAD A DREAM
IN MY MIND IT CAME TO PASS
IF THERE WERE A BLOCKADE
I KNEW IT WOULDN'T LAST

MY DREAM WAS SOMETIMES TEMPERED
IT DIDN'T COME OUT AS I VIEWED
WHEN I PUT IT ALL TOGETHER
IT TURNED OUT SOMEHOW SKEWED

WHEN I HAD ALL MY PARTS IN PLACE
I ASKED THAT OTHERS DO THE SAME
BUT MOST OF THEM WERE MISPLAYED
I GUESS THEY PLAYED A DIFFERENT GAME

NOW THAT I'VE GROWN OLDER
I KNOW I CAN'T CONTROL A TEAM
SO I WILL DO IT ON MY OWN
FOR I HAVE NEVER LOST MY DREAM

NOW ARE YOU HAPPY
by
Joseph Fram

NOW ARE YOU HAPPY
SINCE I'VE CHANGED MY LIFE
HAVING US LIVE TOGETHER
ALMOST AS HUSBAND AND WIFE

YOU MADE ME QUIT LOOKING
FOR SOMETHING UNKNOWN
CAUSE I FOUND IT IN YOU
IT IS SOMETHING HOMEGROWN

NOW ARE YOU HAPPY
GOT ME DOMESTICATED
IT REALLY DOES FIT
IT IS NOT COMPLICATED

WE SEEM TO TRAVEL AROUND
TOGETHER WITH EASE
WITH NO HIDDEN AGENDA
WE DO AS WE PLEASE

SO, NOW ARE YOU HAPPY?
THOUGH YOUR NAME ISN'T FRAM
WELL I REALLY DO HOPE SO
CAUSE, I TELL YOU, I AM

DE JA' VU
by
Joseph Fram

THERE IS NO TIME FOR SECOND THOUGHT
SO OFTEN I'VE BEEN TOLD
WE HAVE NO TIME FOR LOOKING BACK
BEHIND US ASHES, AHEAD GOLD

BUT SOMEHOW I HAVE NEVER FELT
WHAT ALL I'VE HEARD IS TRUE
FOR IF THAT WERE REALLY SO
I'D BE SURPRISED WITH EACH THING NEW

I CANNOT BUT HELP REFLECT
COMPARE MY FUTURE WITH THE PAST
I WONDER EACH NEW THING I DO
IN WHICH MANNER I DID IT LAST

AS I GROW OLDER I CAN SEE
MY LEOPARD SPOTS WILL NEVER CHANGE
AND HOW I AM IS JUST THE SAME
A DIFFERENT PAST WOULD BE SO STRANGE

SO SECOND THOUGHTS ARE A WAY OF LIFE
I HOLD THAT PREMISE TO BE TRUE
AS LIFE GOES ON, IT SEEMS TO ME
I HAVE A CASE OF DE JA' VU

DRIFTING
by
Joseph Fram

I FEAR THAT I AM DRIFTING
AND LONGING FOR THE PAST
WHILE SEEING ALL THE CHANGES
AND HOPING THEY WON'T LAST

I THINK ABOUT THE GOOD OLD DAYS
AND THE TIME THAT I WAS STRONG
WHEN I REALLY HAD THE STRENGTH
TO RIGHT THOSE THINGS GONE WRONG

ALL THOSE THINGS THAT RULED MY LIFE
WERE NEVER IN MY CONTROL
THOUGH I FELT LIKE CENTER STAGE
I ONLY GOT TO PLAY A ROLE

NOW ALL THE THINGS I SAY AND DO
SEEM TO PASS INTO THIN AIR
AND WHEN I LOOK INTO MYSELF
I DON'T KNOW IF I AM THERE

I GUESS I'LL JUST KEEP DRIFTING
TILL I DRIFT OUT OF THE WAY
FOR AFTER ALL IS SAID AND DONE
I MAY NEVER HAVE MY SAY

KINDNESS OF MY MIND
by
Joseph Fram

SHE NEVER WAS THE ROSE
I CREATED HER TO BE
HER THORNS WERE SEEN BY OTHERS
BUT A ROSE SHE WAS TO ME

SHE NEVER REALLY HURT ME
I KEPT TOO MUCH LOVE AROUND
THOUGH I KNEW SHE WASN'T PERFECT
I THOUGHT THE BEST I'D EVER FOUND

I COULD MAKE EXCUSES
WHENEVER THINGS WOULD NOT GO RIGHT
FOR ALL THE LOVE I HAD FOR HER
HID HER WORST FAULTS FROM MY SIGHT

THEN WHEN APART WE DRIFTED
AND I KNEW THE END WAS NEAR
TO LOSE THE LOVE WITHIN MY MIND
BECAME MY GREATEST FEAR

LONG AFTER WE HAD PARTED
THERE IS ONE THING I NOW FIND
THAT ALL THE THINGS I THOUGHT SHE WAS
CAME FROM THE KINDNESS OF MY MIND

BROTHER GEORGE
by
Joseph Fram

HERE'S TO MY LITTLE BROTHER
OF WHOM I'VE ALWAYS BEEN SO PROUD
I AM SURE YOU NEVER HEARD IT
I NEVER SAID IT VERY LOUD

NOW YOU ARE RETIRING
FROM THE WORK YOU DID SO LONG
AS YOU LOOK BACK UPON THE TOIL
THERE WASN'T MUCH THAT WENT SO WRONG

BECAUSE YOU VALUE FAMILY
YOU HAVE BEEN LOYAL TO THE END
GOD WATCHES WHAT HIS CHILDREN DO
AND HE WILL GUIDE YOU ROUND THE BEND

LIFE WILL ALWAYS BE A CHALLENGE
GETTING US FROM HERE TO THERE
BUT AS LONG AS THERE IS PEACE INSIDE
HAPPINESS GROWS YEAR BY YEAR

THERE ARE SOME THINGS I MIGHT HAVE MISSED
IN THE YEARS IN WHICH YOU GREW
BUT ONE THING ALWAYS STAYED THE SAME
AND THAT'S THE CHILDHOOD LOVE WE KNEW

LOVE FOR CHRISTMAS
by
Joseph Fram

IT SEEMED JUST ANOTHER CHRISTMAS
AS I SHOPPED IN EVERY STORE
WHEN I THOUGHT THAT I WAS DONE
I REMEMBERED JUST ONE MORE

THERE ARE MANY THINGS TO BUY
AND SO MANY DREAMS TO FILL
EACH HAS MADE A CHRISTMAS WISH
A SECRET THEY KEEP STILL

FOR THEY BELIEVE THAT SANTA CLAUS
WILL KNOW WHAT'S ON THEIR MIND
AND HE WILL NEVER STOP HIS SEARCH
UNTIL THEIR TOY HE'LL FIND

IT COULD BE SOMETHING THAT THEY SAW
LAST SUMMER AS THEY PLAYED
SOMETHING WE HAVE LONG FORGOT
YET IN THEIR MIND IT STAYED

SINCE I COULDN'T READ THEIR THOUGHTS
I PRAYED FOR GUIDANCE FROM ABOVE
THEN I SAW HIM SMILE AT ME
AND SAY "JUST GIVE THEM LOVE"

HER WORDS
by
Joseph Fram

WHAT WE HAD IS OVER
ARE WORDS SHE SAID TO ME
BUT YOU JUST KEEP HANGING ON
YOU REFUSE TO SET ME FREE

WHAT MIGHT HAVE BEEN IS GONE
I NO LONGER CARE FOR YOU
YOU CAN NEVER CHANGE MY MIND
NO MATTER WHAT YOU SAY OR DO

I HAVE NO SHAME FOR WHAT I DID
AND NO SORROW FOR MY DEED
I'VE GROWN TIRED OF YOUR LOVE
AND MUST FULFILL MY EVERY NEED

YOU WILL SOON GET OVER ME
JUST PRETEND THAT I HAVE DIED
LET ME BLAME IT ALL ON YOU
FOR, THEN, TO ME, I HAVE NOT LIED

NOW YOUR WORDS MAKE SENSE TO ME
BUT IT IS YOU WHO WILL NOT LET GO
DIDN'T TALK SHOWS TELL YOU HOW
WELL, PERHAPS THEY JUST DON'T KNOW

MY FATHER'S SON
by
Joseph Fram

I AM MY FATHER'S SON
HE KNOWS ALL THINGS I DO
I WILL HAVE MY UPS AND DOWNS
HE KNOWS IT IS NOTHING NEW

SOMETIMES HE SEES ME ANGRY
THIS HE HAS SEEN BEFORE
AND THE WORST I COULD BE
HE'S SEEN MANY TIMES AND MORE

WHEN THERE IS SORROW IN MY SOUL
HE REACHES OUT TO ME
SORROW'S JUST THE OTHER SIDE
OF HAPPINESS, YOU SEE

WHEN HE HEARS MY LAUGHTER
HE WILL JOIN ME FOR A WHILE
THOUGH I HAVE NEVER SEEN IT
WHEN HE LEAVES I FEEL HIS SMILE

YES, I AM MY FATHER'S SON
I WILL NEVER BE WHAT HE CAN BE
I DON'T THINK THAT'S WHAT HE WANTS
HE'S JUST HAPPY IF I AM ME

CHRISTMAS I REMEMBER
by
Joseph Fram

THE CHRISTMAS I REMEMBER
WAS FILLED WITH LOVE AND JOY
WITH HAPPINESS CHRISTMAS MORN
FOR EVERY GIRL AND BOY

IT WASN'T ALL THE THINGS WE GOT
IT WAS THE LOVE OF GIVING THEN
JUST TO SHARE A LITTLE PRESENT
I WISH IT WERE THAT WAY AGAIN

WE DIDN'T HAVE TO CHANGE OUR WAYS
TO RISK GETTING NOTHING DUE TO FEAR
I REMEMBER THAT OUR CHRISTMAS FACE
WAS THE ONE WE WORE ALL YEAR

NOW THE YEARS GO MARCHING BY
CHRISTMAS CHANGES WITH THE TIME
BUT I WOULD LIKE TO CHANGE IT BACK
TO THE CHRISTMAS THAT WAS MINE

I KNOW I CAN'T GO BACK IN TIME
AND WOULDN'T IF I COULD
IF I COULD CHANGE ONE SEPTEMBER DAY
THAT'S THE FIRST THING THAT I WOULD

SEPT. 11, 2001

ONE SUMMER NIGHT
by
Joseph Fram

I STAYED UP LATE ONE SUMMER NIGHT
SEARCHING FOR MY GUIDING STAR
ALL THE WORLDLY THINGS I LEFT BEHIND
IN MY MIND I TRAVELED FAR

FOR THAT NIGHT IT TOOK ME
PLACES THAT I HAD NEVER BEEN
IT WAS A NIGHT OF PEACEFULNESS
I KNEW I COULD CALL BACK AGAIN

ALL MY LIFE I HAVE BEEN PLANTED
IN A WORLD OF WORK AND SWEAT
AND THE MORE I TRY TO GET AHEAD
THE FARTHER BEHIND I GET

I CAN'T CHANGE THE WAY THINGS WORK
IT IS NOT ALL THAT BAD FOR ME
I CAN ALWAYS USE MY MIND
TO PUT ME WHERE I LONG TO BE

LATELY EVERY NOW AND THEN
WHEN I WANT TO GET AWAY
I THINK ABOUT THAT SUMMER NIGHT
IN MY MIND THAT'S WHERE I'LL STAY

HARD TIMES
by
Joseph Fram

WHEN IT IS EASY SAILING
IT IS EASY TO BE KIND
LOVE CAN FLOW SO EASILY
AND NO FAULTS DO YOU FIND

SOMETIMES WHEN ROADS ARE ROCKY
YOU EXCHANGE A WORD OR TWO
THEN THERE IS THE MAKING UP
AND KNOWING WHAT TO DO

THEN THERE IS EASY GLIDING
WHEN NOT MUCH NEED BE SAID
AND MOST IS PEACE AND HAPPINESS
AND TRANQUILITY INSTEAD

ONCE IN A WHILE A STALL OR TWO
WHEN NOTHING SEEMS TO GO
IT IS AT THESE TIMES
YOU NEED EACH OTHER SO

AND AT TIMES THERE IS DISASTER
WHEN RELATIONSHIPS ARE MARRED
THAT'S THE TIMES TO STICK TOGETHER
WHEN THE TIMES ARE REALLY HARD

NOT FOR SALE
by
Joseph Fram

THIS MAN IS NOT FOR SALE
HE'S PAID A HIGH PRICE FOR HIS NAME
HE WILL FREELY GIVE HIS LOVE
TO HIM IT IS NOT A GAME

LOVE IS EVERYTHING HE HAS
BUT TWO MUST SHARE FOR IT TO GROW
THOUGH OTHERS CANNOT FEEL THE BLISS
THERE IS NO NEED FOR THEM TO KNOW

YOUR MOTHER'S LOVE WAS WAITING THERE
FOR ONE TO TOUCH AND MAKE IT LIVE
SHE TRIED BEFORE BUT ALL IN VAIN
THEY ALWAYS TOOK BUT DID NOT GIVE

SO DEAR CHILD WE WAITED LONG
A SEARCH WELL INTO LATER YEARS
LET US NOW ENJOY OUR LOVE
WE PAID THE PRICE IN EARLY TEARS

YOUR MOTHER DID NOT SHOP FOR ME
THINK WHAT YOU MAY ABOUT US TWO
THE ONLY WAY TO HOLD THIS HEART
ARE SIMPLE WORDS OF "I LOVE YOU"

MY CHILDREN
by
Joseph Fram

SWEET CHILDREN SAT BESIDE ME
WHILE WE WERE AT THE OCEAN SIDE
THEIR SMILES WERE SO BRILLIANT
AND THEIR BEAUTY COULD NOT HIDE

WHEN THEY PUT THEIR HANDS IN MINE
THEY MAKE ME FEEL JUST LIKE A KING
WHEN CHILDREN'S LAUGHTER FILLS THE AIR
IT EVEN MAKES A SAD HEART SING

WHEN THERE ARE CHILDREN IN YOUR LIFE
YOU CAN BECOME A CHILD TOO
AND ALL THE GAMES YOU USED TO PLAY
ARE THINGS AGAIN THAT YOU CAN DO

LIKE PLAYING HIGH UPON A SWING
OR A GAME OF HIDE AND SEEK
REMEMBER WHEN YOU CLOSE YOUR EYES
YOU ARE NOT ALLOWED TO PEEK

SO ISN'T BEING CHILDREN FUN
NO MATTER WHAT YOUR AGE
YOU CAN DO ALL THE THINGS THEY DO
WHEN ALL THE WORLD'S YOUR STAGE

NOSES
by
Joseph Fram

WHEN GOD GAVE US NOSES
IN THE MIDDLE OF OUR FACE
IT WAS NOT BY ACCIDENT
HE PUT THEM IN THE RIGHT PLACE

NOTICE YOUR EYES ARE BEHIND THEM
PLACED TO SEARCH FAR AND WIDE
AND WITH THE NOSE IN THE MIDDLE
YOU CAN USE IT AS A GUIDE

IT IS ONLY NOT FOR BEAUTY
OR TO SMELL THE DIFFERENT THINGS
NOR TO CATCH A COLD IN WINTER
OR THE REDNESS THAT IT BRINGS

FOR YOU SEE, GOD PUT HIS BEAUTY
IN EVERYTHING HE DID
HE INTENDED IT FOR VIEWING
AND NOT TO HAVE IT HID

SO WHEN YOU ARE WITHIN GOD'S BEAUTY
YOU SHOULD LOOK BEYOND YOUR NOSES
IF YOU DISREGARD THE THORNS
AND CONCENTRATE ON THE ROSES

NOT ALL GEMS ARE DIAMONDS
by
Joseph Fram

GOD HAS CREATED MANY THINGS
FOR ALL OUR EYES TO SEE
WE SHOULD PICK THE ONES WE LIKE
AND LET THE OTHERS BE

FOR SOME MAY LIKE TO LOOK
AT BEAUTY THAT IS JUST SKIN DEEP
AND OTHERS FIND NATURE'S FLAWS
THAT THEY ARE CONTENT TO KEEP

FOR IN THIS WORLD OF MANY THINGS
WE EACH CAN PICK AND CHOOSE
IF WE ARE CONTENT WITH WHAT WE HAVE
THEN THERE IS NOTHING WE CAN LOSE

MOST ALL THE THINGS THAT WE TRY
WE DO THE BEST WE CAN
IF OTHERS SEE THE FLAWS IN US
WHAT WE DID IS BETTER THAN

SO NOT ALL GEMS ARE DIAMONDS
BUT DIAMONDS DO NOT RULE THE EARTH
FOR EACH STONE IS PRECIOUS
AND EACH OWNER KNOWS ITS WORTH

FUNNY
by
Joseph Fram

FUNNY HOW IT SEEMS SO STRANGE
NOW THAT I'VE HAD SOME TIME FOR THOUGHT
ABOUT THE TIME I HELD ON TO LOVE
I THOUGHT I HAD BUT I DID NOT

THE LOVE I HAD WENT JUST ONE WAY
BUT I CLUNG TO IT SO TIGHT
WITH NOT SO MUCH A SECOND THOUGHT
THAT ONE WAY LOVE IS JUST NOT RIGHT

WITH ALL THE THINGS SHE'D SAY AND DO
I THOUGHT IT MUST BE JUST HER STYLE
FOR SHE WAS ALL THINGS DEAR TO ME
'TWAS NOT JUST A MISS BUT BY A MILE

FOR THE MIND PLAYS FUNNY TRICKS
WHEN YOU'RE IN LOVE WHAT DO YOU CARE
ABOUT ALL THE FUNNY THINGS THEY DO
JUST AS LONG AS THEY ARE ALWAYS THERE

FUNNY HOW THE HEART ADJUSTS
NOW TO THINK HOW HARD I FOUGHT
TO HOLD ON TO ONE SO TIGHTLY
WHO NOW IS JUST AN AFTERTHOUGHT

CHRISTMAS IMAGE
by
Joseph Fram

IMAGINE A CHRISTMAS
IN WHICH CHRIST WOULD LIVE
WITH A WORLD FULL OF LOVE
FOR US TO TAKE AND GIVE

WHERE ALL THE WORLD'S PEOPLE
WERE KIND TO EACH OTHER
AND FORGAVE US OUR SINS
LIKE TRUE SISTER AND BROTHER

WHERE ALL UNKIND DEEDS
WERE DONE BY MISTAKE
AND A LESSON WAS LEARNED
WHEN HOLY GRACE CAME AWAKE

AND IF ONE GOT HURT
ALL WOULD COME TO HIS AID
AND THEIR PAYMENT WAS LOVE
FOR THE EFFORT THEY MADE

IMAGINE A CHRISTMAS
THAT LASTS A LONG WHILE
THEN PICTURE CHRIST WATCHING
AND IMAGINE HIS SMILE

DEATH
by
Joseph Fram

DEATH IS ONLY NATURAL
FOR EACH THERE IS A CALL
RICH AND POOR AND GREAT ONES
IT WILL EVENTUALLY GET US ALL

MOST WHO ARE STILL LIVING
ENJOY EACH DAY BY DAY
THEY HAVE LITTLE TIME TO THINK
OF WHEN THEY WILL GO AWAY

SOME ARE OBSESSED WITH DYING
AND LOOK FORWARD TO THE END
THEY KEEP LOOKING TOWARD THE GRAVEYARD
AND CAN NEVER SEE AROUND THE BEND

WHILE MOST KEEP A PERSPECTIVE
THEY KNOW THEY WILL NEVER WIN
THEIR LIVES ARE GOOD AND PROPER
AND TRY TO KEEP AWAY FROM SIN

SOMETIMES DEATH IS A TRAGEDY
WE THINK ALL WE KNOW ARE LIES
WE WILL NEVER KNOW THE REASON
WHEN A CHILD DIES

EASIER NOW
by
Joseph Fram

I SAW HER NOT TOO LONG AGO
AFTER MANY, MANY YEARS
THE ONE WHO BROKE MY HEART
AND LEFT ME AWASH IN TEARS

WE SMILED AND SPOKE AS WE MET
AND TRIED OUR BEST TO CARE
THERE WERE WORDS IN MY MIND
SAYING I SHOULD NOT BE THERE

I REMEMBER WHEN SHE LEFT ME
WITH ANOTHER FOR TO BE
SAYING I HAD BEEN NICE TO HER
BUT SHE DID NOT WANT TO BE WITH ME

THOSE WORDS RANG IN MY MIND
AND WERE SO HARD TO FORGET
EVEN NOW ONCE IN A WHILE
I STILL THINK OF THEM YET

AND THEN WHEN I SAW HER
HER WORDS CAME BACK TO ME SOMEHOW
BUT SINCE THE PAIN IS LONG GONE
IT IS MUCH EASIER FOR ME NOW

LONG GOOD MORNING
by
Joseph Fram

I KNOW THIS HERE FRIENDLY FELLA
I SEE HIM MOST EVERY DAY
I NEVER KNEW A SINGLE PERSON
COULD HAVE SO MANY THINGS TO SAY

HE'LL CATCH ME IN EARLY MORNING
WITH SOME STORY HE JUST HEARD
I NEVER GET JUST THE ESSENCE
HE WILL TELL ME EVERY WORD

HE MUST ENJOY WHAT HE IS SAYING
HE THINKS THAT I DO TOO
BUT I JUST STAND AND LISTEN
FOR THERE IS NOTHING ELSE TO DO

IF I TRY TO GET A WORD IN EDGEWISE
HE IS QUICK TO BLOCK MY SAY
HE THINKS I HAVE NOTHING BETTER TO DO
THAN LISTEN TO HIM TALK ALL DAY

I REALLY HATE TO SAY GOOD MORNING
AND I AM GOING TO TELL HIM SOON
THAT A GOOD MORNING GREETING
REALLY SHOULD NOT LAST TILL NOON

LEADERS TAKE THE BLAME
by
Joseph Fram

I REALLY LOVE MY COUNTRY
BUT I HAVE GROWN AFRAID
OF THE POWER OF OUR LEADERS
FOR THE MISTAKES THEY HAVE MADE

OUR WEAPONS ARE SO POWERFUL
AND OUR LEADERS INSIST
CIVILIAN CASUALTIES ARE JUSTIFIED
WHEN LAUNCHED MISSILES MISS

AND OF COURSE THEY CANNOT TELL US
WHY THEY BOMB A MEDICAL FACILITY
THE REASON MUST BE HIGHLY SECRET
LEST WE BREACH NATIONAL SECURITY

WHAT REALLY IS MOST SENSELESS
AND GIVES ME AN AWFUL FIT
IS RELEASING RANDOM BOMBS
IN HOPES SOME TERRORIST WILL BE HIT

"WAG THE DOG" LOOKS LIKE IT MAKES SENSE
AS OUR LEADERS TRY TO HIDE THEIR SHAME
IT IS SAD THAT BY THEIR ACTIONS
THEY PUT ALL AMERICANS TO BLAME

HAPPY BIRTHDAY DOREEN
by
Joseph Fram

THERE WAS SOMETHING SPECIAL
WAY BACK IN NINETEEN THIRTY-TWO
IN JUNE THAT YEAR A BOY WAS BORN
AND IN SEPTEMBER THERE WAS YOU

THERE MUST HAVE BEEN SOME MAGIC
IN THE AIR FOR THAT WHOLE YEAR
FOR IT TOOK US UP AND DOWN
BUT IT ALSO BROUGHT US HERE

THAT MAGIC HAD SOME OTHER THINGS
LIKE HONESTY, LOYALTY AND PRIDE
AND TO FACE UP TO OUR TASKS
NOT TO RUN AND HIDE

AND IT GAVE US BOTH A CHANCE
TO TRY LOVE A DIFFERENT WAY
SO THE LOVE THAT WE HAVE NOW
WOULD BE STRONG ENOUGH TO STAY

SO HAPPY BIRTHDAY SWEETHEART
I GIVE MY LOVE TO YOU
AND THIS LOVE I GIVE YOU NOW
I SAVED SINCE NINETEEN THIRTY-TWO

I'LL WAIT FOR YOU
by
Joseph Fram

A GENTLE SMILE FROM A FRIEND TO ALL
AND KINDNESS WHEN YOU TOUCH HIS HAND
HE'LL NOT REGRET THE LIFE HE LIVED
FOR LONG AGO HE TAMED HIS LAND

HE WAS ONCE ALONE OUT THERE
AND LEARNED THAT NATURE IS YOUR FRIEND
HE LEARNED TO LOVE ALL CREATURES THEN
I GUESS HE WILL UNTIL THE END

HE TELLS OF HARDSHIPS LONG AGO
BUT NEVER ONCE WILL HE COMPLAIN
FOR HE HAD LOVE THROUGHOUT THOSE YEARS
AND SOON HE'LL SEE HER ONCE AGAIN

HE SHOWS YOU PRIZES THAT THEY SHARED
EACH PLACED WITH LOVE HE CAN'T FORGET
HE SOMETIMES SEES HER STANDING THERE
THOUGH LONG AGO SHE DIED, AND YET

THEIR LOVE WAS STRONG ENOUGH TO LAST
THERE IS NO DEATH WHEN LOVE IS TRUE
FOR IN HIS MIND SHE'LL ALWAYS LIVE
AND HEARS HER SAY "I'LL WAIT FOR YOU"

LOVE PLUS
by
Joseph Fram

WHEN I TRY TO DESCRIBE IT
IT WON'T SOUND LIKE LOVE
HOW DO YOU TALK ABOUT FEELINGS
THAT COME FROM ABOVE

LOVE IS SOMETHING THAT'S SENT
SO MANKIND CAN ENDURE
THERE IS NO NEED TO ADD
TO SOMETHING SO PURE

SOMETIMES MAN IS NOT HAPPY
JUST TO KNOW LOVE IS THERE
WHEN HE TRIES TO DESCRIBE IT
HE MUST LOOK EVERYWHERE

THOSE WITH SOME WISDOM
WHO LOOK LONG AND HARD
WILL FIND LOVE IS WAITING
IN THEIR MIND'S OWN BACKYARD

THEN THEY WILL TALK ALL AROUND IT
AND TELL HOW THEY CARE
WHEN THEY TRY TO DESCRIBE LOVE
WHAT'S LEFT IS "YOU HAVE TO BE THERE"

JUST FOR FUN
by
Joseph Fram

IT IS SO IMPORTANT
WE MUST DO THIS TODAY
WE MUST KEEP THIS APPOINTMENT
WHAT WILL PEOPLE SAY

I SAW THESE FRIENDS THE OTHER DAY
TO THE THEATER WE MUST GO
IT REALLY DOESN'T MATTER
THAT WE HAVE ALREADY SEEN THE SHOW

IF WE DO NOT HURRY
WE MISS THE IMPORTANT THINGS IN LIFE
MISSING ALL THESE NEEDY THINGS
WILL BRING AGONY, TEARS AND STRIFE

IN BETWEEN I HAVE BEEN THINKING
WHY WE ALWAYS HAVE TO HAVE A PLAN
THERE ARE OTHER THINGS TO DO
AND THOSE I'LL BET WE CAN

HOW ABOUT SPUR OF THE MOMENT
AND STOP THIS FURIOUS RUN
WHY CAN'T WE KEEP THINGS SIMPLE
AND DO THINGS JUST FOR FUN

MYRNA FAREWELL
by
Joseph Fram

WELL, HERE YOU GO MYRNA
OFF TO A DIFFERENT NEW LIFE
ONE THAT WILL INCLUDE FAMILY
LIKE GRANDMOTHER AND WIFE

THE DUTY BEHIND YOU
YOUR LEGACY WE SEE
FOR WITHOUT YOUR FINE EFFORT
LORD KNOWS WHERE WE'D BE

FROM A SMALL ROOM IN A CORNER
TO WHERE WE ARE NOW
WE KNEW IT IMPOSSIBLE
BUT YOU MANAGED SOMEHOW

AND NOW WE WILL CHERISH
ALL THE WORK YOU HAVE DONE
FROM DEEP IN OUR HEARTS
WE SAY "THANKS" FROM EACH ONE

SO NOW RETIRE IN PEACE
AND BE PROUD OF YOUR DEED
FROM THE BEST WE CAN OFFER
IS GOD BLESS AND GOD SPEED

GOD'S RELIGION
by
Joseph Fram

I REALLY CAN'T REMEMBER
WHEN GOD PUT US ON THIS EARTH
THAT HE GAVE US ONE RELIGION
WE ALL SHARED AT OUR BIRTH

HE SAID SOMETHING ABOUT CHOICES
BUT WHEN WAS RELIGION INTRODUCED?
I THINK IF IT WERE UP TO HIM
THE TERM WOULD NEVER HAVE A USE

IF I RECALL MY HISTORY
RELIGION HAS PLAYED MOST EVERY PART
OF EVERY WAR SINCE TIME BEGAN
AND FOR EACH NEW WAR TO START

GOD SAID TO LOVE YOUR FELLOW MAN
NOT TRY TO BEND THEM TO YOUR WILL
IF THEY DO NOT BELIEVE AS YOU
IS THAT A REASON YOU SHOULD KILL?

FOR THOSE WHO IGNORE THE LOVE
EACH RELIGION HAS TO GIVE
GOD DOESN'T ASK YOU KILL THEIRS
SO THE ONE YOU HAVE WILL LIVE

BETTER PLACE DOWN THE ROAD
by
Joseph Fram

SEEMS THAT WHEN I GET A JOB DONE
OR PICK A PLACE TO STAY
THERE IS ALWAYS SOME DISSATISFACTION
I AM TOLD THERE IS A BETTER WAY

I THOUGHT IF YOU WERE DOING SOMETHING
YOU SHOULD KNOW WHEN YOU ARE THROUGH
BUT NOW I JUST WAIT FOR SOME OUTSIDER
TO COME AND TELL ME WHAT TO DO

IT'S NOT THAT THEY ARE SMARTER
THEY JUST HAVE TO HAVE THEIR SAY
SO NO MATTER HOW I DO THINGS
THEY CRITICIZE TO MAKE THEIR DAY

THEN SURELY THEY WILL LEAVE ME
AND HELP ME NOT A WIT
THEY MUMBLE AS I DO THE WORK
WHILE ON THEIR RUMP THEY SIT

SO LATELY WHEN I DO THINGS
I GET HALF DONE AND THEN HOLD
I FOLD MY ARMS AND WAIT TO HEAR
'BOUT A BETTER PLACE DOWN THE ROAD

BITTER WORDS
by
Joseph Fram

WHEN ONE ENCOUNTERS BITTERNESS
IT IS BEST NOT TO SAY A WORD
NO MATTER WHAT OTHER WORDS MAY FOLLOW
IT IS THE BITTER ONE THAT IS HEARD

WHEN ONE SAYS THEY ARE SORRY
MOSTLY THEY TRULY ARE
BUT THE DAMAGE THAT HAS BEEN DONE
IN THEIR LIVES WILL CARRY FAR

WHO OF US WILL EVER KNOW
THE SCARS THAT WE IMPART
WE CAN'T SEE THEM ON THE SKIN
WE DON'T SEE INSIDE THE HEART

SO WHEN A LOVE OR FRIENDSHIP
SEEMS TO FALL APART
IT MIGHT HAVE BEEN THOSE BITTER WORDS
THAT CAUSED IT ALL TO START

BITTER WORDS ARE BEST UNSAID
EVEN IF THEY CROSS YOUR MIND
IT IS NOT WORTH THE HURT YOU CAUSE
YOU'RE BOTH BETTER OFF YOU'LL FIND

CHRISTMAS TIME LOVE
by
Joseph Fram

WHEN CHRISTMAS COMES AGAIN THIS YEAR
THE COUNT FOR US IS NUMBER THREE
THE TIME HAS GONE SO QUICKLY BY
AND YOU ARE STILL IN LOVE WITH ME

TIME STOOD STILL THE DAY WE MET
AND LOVE TOOK ITS PLACE
NOW WHEN MY MIND SEEKS PARADISE
I SEE YOUR LOVELY FACE

CHRISTMAS IS A SPECIAL TIME
A TIME TO THANK THE CHRISTMAS STAR
IT WILL SHINE THROUGHOUT THE YEAR
AND KEEP ME CLOSE TO WHERE YOU ARE

CHRISTMAS IS A TIME TO GIVE
FOR CHRISTMAS LOVE IS ALL AROUND
HOW WELL I KNOW THAT THIS IS TRUE
'TWAS CHRISTMASTIME WHEN YOU I FOUND

HOW MANY?
by
Joseph Fram

HOW MANY MEN WILL HAVE TO DIE
HOW LONG WILL WE HAVE TO FIGHT
AND IF WELL KEEP KILLING EACH OTHER
WHEN WILL WE DECLARE IT RIGHT

I GUESS IF YOU DON'T DECLARE A WAR
SOMEHOW THE COUNTRY THINKS YOU WEAK
AND FOR THOSE WHO BELIEVE IN PEACE
THEY MUST NOT BE ALLOWED TO SPEAK

IT REALLY MUST NOT MATTER
HOW MANY YOUNG SOLDIERS DIE
POLITICIANS CALL YOU TRAITORS
IF YOU EVEN QUESTION WHY

I DON'T SEE THE POLITICIANS
PUTTING ON ANY UNIFORM
WHILE THEY DIRECT OTHERS' DEATH
AT HOME AND KEEPING WARM

WHEN POLITICIANS GET RICH ENOUGH
THEY MAY DECIDE TO TAKE A BREAK
AND QUIT KILLING ALL OUR YOUNG ONES
FOR ALL THE GRIEVING MOTHERS' SAKE

BEEN LOVED?
by
Joseph Fram

WHEN SOMEONE SAYS THEY LOVE YOU
CAN YOU KNOW WHAT THEY FEEL INSIDE
IS IT JUST WORDS THEY ARE SAYING
OR IS THERE A RAGING TIDE?

HOW DO YOU DEFINE A LOVE
IS IT ACTION OR A WORD
IS THERE AN INNER SENSE
OR SOMETHING ONE HAS HEARD

DON'T YOU THINK IF LOVE IS REAL
THEN ALL THE THINGS WE SAY
ARE SOMETIMES WINDOW-DRESSING
AND JUST GET IN THE WAY

FOR IF LOVE IS REALLY TRUE
SHOULD IT NOT SHOW UP IN DEEDS
LIKE WHEN YOU'RE FEELING REALLY LOW
SHOULD IT FULFILL ALL OF YOUR NEEDS

THE SADDEST THING I HAVE EVER HEARD
I KNOW YOU FEEL THAT WAY TOO
NOT KNOWING IF YOU HAVE BEEN LOVED
AND IF THAT LOVE WAS TRUE

GOD'S CHURCH
by
Joseph Fram

THERE IS PEACE AT LAST
WITH THE WORLD SHUT OUTSIDE
IN THIS QUIET LITTLE CHURCH
WHERE GOD WILL LET YOU HIDE

HE ALLOWS ANYONE TO ENTER
SOMETIMES MANY, SOMETIMES FEW
AND HE WILL ALWAYS HEAR YOU
NO MATTER THE LOCATION OF THE PEW

THERE ARE LITTLE ELDERLY LADIES
AND A MIXTURE OF SOME MEN
THEIR GLANCES TELL YOU WELCOME
PLEASE COME AGAIN AND AGAIN

SOME ARE VERY BUSY
WITH THE ASSIGNMENTS THAT THEY DO
AND THEY SHOW SUCH INTENSE DEVOTION
EVEN AFTER THE SERVICE IS THROUGH

WE ARE THERE FOR DIFFERENT REASONS
SEEKING GOD'S PEACE IN THE SUN
IT IS THERE FOR THAT MOMENT
HE PUTS HIS HAND ON EVERYONE

IT DOESN'T MATTER NOW
by
Joseph Fram

JUST WHAT IS THE POINT
I KEEP ASKING MYSELF
TO REMEMBER DETAILS
SITTING ON MY MIND'S SHELF

ARE THERE MEMORIES
THAT I PUT THERE TO LAST
DO THEY MAKE A DIFFERENCE NOW
OR ONLY EMBRACE THE PAST

IF I MADE A DIFFERENCE
WILL SOMEONE REMEMBER ME
IF NO ONE REMEMBERS
JUST A MARK IN TIME I'LL BE

WHO WOULD STORE MEMORIES
OF A LIFE SO PLAIN
IS THERE ANY USE NOW
TO TRY TO RELIVE IT AGAIN

I TALK OF MEMORIES THAT I HAVE
TO SHOW SOME OTHERS HOW
BUT WHAT I SEE IN THEIR EYES
IS "IT DOESN'T MATTER NOW"

TIME AND DISTANCE
by
Joseph Fram

SOMEHOW TIME AND DISTANCE
CURE A BROKEN HEART
THOUGH IT DOESN'T SEEM SO
WHEN THE HEARTACHES START

ALL THE THINGS BEFORE YOU
THAT ONCE YOU HELD SO DEAR
SEEM TO FADE INTO THE AIR
WHEN THEY ARE NOT NEAR

THERE ARE THINGS YOU HOLD ON TO
SO YOU DON'T LOSE YOUR MIND
BUT ALSO THERE ARE NEW THINGS
GOD PUT THERE FOR YOU TO FIND

SO WHEN YOU'RE HURTING BADLY
AND THE TEARS JUST FALL LIKE RAIN
TRY TO TAKE SOME TIME AND DISTANCE
TO HELP YOU EASE THE PAIN

GOD DOESN'T WANT YOU TO HURT FOR LONG
THAT IS WHY HE PUT SOME SPACE ON EARTH
IF YOU MOVE YOUR TROUBLES FROM THE PAIN
YOU WILL SEE WHAT IT IS WORTH

MY SAY
by
Joseph Fram

THE WORDS FLOWED LIKE WATER
THRU DAY, DARK AND MORN
IT SEEMS I'VE BEEN TALKING
SINCE THE DAY I WAS BORN

AT TIMES I MADE A POINT
AND SOME WERE VERY CLEVER
SOME WOULD MAKE A DIFFERENCE
AND OTHERS THAT WOULD NEVER

I TRIED TO PUT SOME WORDS DOWN
THAT I THOUGHT PERHAPS WERE NEW
AND SADLY COME TO REALIZE
THAT THEY ARE VERY FEW

I KNOW THAT I HAVE SPOKEN MUCH
AND WRITTEN SOME THINGS DOWN
HOW MANY OF MY SPEECHES
REMAIN WHEN I AM NOT AROUND

HOW MANY PEOPLE LISTENED
AND DID I HAVE MY WAY
THE THING THAT BOTHERS ME THE MOST
I MAY NOT HAVE HAD MY SAY

Are you ready for the next step
in Joseph's Journey?

Coming soon -- Volume 3!

I hope you enjoyed reading my poetry.
You may write to me at the address below.
                                    Joe Fram

Everlasting Publishing
P.O. Box 1061
Yakima, WA 98907

www.ingramcontent.com/pod-product-compliance
Lightning Source LLC
Chambersburg PA
CBHW071732020426
42331CB00008B/2001